ELIZABETH BARRETT BROWNING

¶ Elizabeth Barrett Browning was born on 6 March 1806, at Coxhoe Hall in Durham. She died in Florence on 29 June 1861.

ELIZABETH   BARRETT   BROWNING
from a chalk drawing by FIELD TALFOURD (1859)
National Portrait Gallery

ELIZABETH BARRETT BROWNING

by

ALETHEA HAYTER

PUBLISHED FOR
THE BRITISH COUNCIL
AND THE NATIONAL BOOK LEAGUE
BY LONGMANS, GREEN & CO

LONGMANS, GREEN & CO LTD
Longman House, Burnt Mill, Harlow, Essex

*Associated companies, branches and
representatives throughout the world*

*First published 1965
Reprinted with additions to bibliography 1969*
© Alethea Hayter 1965

*Printed in Great Britain by
F. Mildner & Sons, London, EC1*

ELIZABETH BARRETT BROWNING

I

WHEN Wordsworth died, just half way through the nineteenth century, and a successor for him as Poet Laureate had to be found, the claims of Elizabeth Barrett Browning to succeed him were seriously canvassed. It was suggested that a female Poet Laureate would be particularly suitable when a woman was on the throne of England; but the influential *Athenaeum* flatly stated that in any case no living poet of either sex had a higher claim than Mrs Browning's. This seems to us a startling pronouncement to have been made on the same day—1 June 1850—on which *In Memoriam* was published. Tennyson in fact got the Laureateship, to Mrs Browning's satisfaction though she had thought Leigh Hunt ought to have it; not even she had thought of Browning as a possible candidate.

The suggestion that a female Sovereign should have a female Poet Laureate seemed foolish enough to Mrs Browning. She thought of herself as a poet, not a poetess; she considered that poetry should be judged by its merits, not by the sex of its writers. 'When I talk of women, I do not speak of them . . . according to a separate, peculiar and womanly standard, but according to the common standard of human nature', she said. But it has never been possible for critics to disentangle Mrs Browning from her sex. She was always being classed by her contemporaries as the top woman poet (generally bracketed with Sappho), not simply as a good, or very good, or fairly good, poet. No such woman writer would probably come again for a millennium, wrote Sydney Dobell unprophetically in 1850; but he went on to say that no woman writer, not even Mrs Browning, would ever write a great poem. 'She was a woman of real genius, I know; but what is the upshot of it all? She and her sex had better mind the kitchen and the children', said FitzGerald. Elizabeth Barrett Browning was as much obscured as a poet by her sex and her personal legend as Byron was by his. It is therefore difficult to assess her achievement as objectively as that of other nineteenth-century poets such as Patmore, or Clough, or Meredith, with whom she might reasonably be classed; but she has in fact much more in common with them than with Christina Rossetti or Emily Brontë.

II

Elizabeth Barrett was born on 6 March 1806 at Coxhoe Hall in Durham. She was the eldest of the twelve children of Edward Moulton Barrett and his wife Mary. When she was three years old, the family moved to Hope End in Hereford-shire, and she spent the next twenty-three years of her life in this minaretted country house overlooking a lake and deep in a wooded park. Here she produced her *juvenilia: The Battle of Marathon*, an epic poem written when she was thirteen and privately printed by her father in 1820; *An Essay on Mind, with other Poems*, published in 1826; a number of poems published in magazines; and a good deal of verse, including one long poem 'The Development of Genius', which remained unpublished in her lifetime. Encouraged by two neighbours, the scholars Hugh Stuart Boyd and Uvedale Price, she made a thorough study of Classical and Byzantine Greek literature, and of prosody. Apart from a severe but unidentified illness in 1821, she led a normal social and family life during all these years.

In 1832 financial losses forced her father to sell Hope End and move with his children (his wife had died in 1828) first to Sidmouth, in Devonshire, and then in 1835 to London. In 1833 Elizabeth Barrett published a volume containing a translation of the *Prometheus Bound* of Aeschylus, and some short poems, but neither this nor her earlier volumes (all published anonymously) attracted much notice. Her first real success was achieved with *The Seraphim, and other Poems*, published in 1838 under her own name, which was given long and mainly favourable reviews in the leading journals.

The literary scene on which Elizabeth Barrett entered in the late 1830s was comparatively empty—an undistinguished pause between two great periods of creative writing. Wordsworth, Leigh Hunt and Landor were the patriarchs of the day, but their best work was past; Tennyson, Browning, Dickens, Carlyle had published their first works, but their great achievement and fame were still to come; Thackeray, Ruskin and the Brontës were still just below the literary horizon. The admired writers of the day were Talfourd, Harriet Martineau, Harrison Ainsworth, Mary Russell Mitford, Thomas Hood, Bulwer Lytton, Barry Cornwall, Mrs Hemans, Letitia Landon, Sheridan Knowles. Among these writers Elizabeth Barrett began to make friends and a place for herself. Her ill-health and her family circumstances prevented her from going out much into the social life of London, but she embarked on exchanges of letters with literary figures which were to influence both her writing and her life. Among her correspondents were Wordsworth, Edgar Allan Poe, Carlyle, Harriet Martineau, Mary Russell Mitford (who gave her Flush, her spaniel), John Kenyon, R. H. Horne and the painter Benjamin Robert Haydon. They exchanged criticisms and appreciations of each other's work, discussed other writers of the day and the ethics and techniques of their profession; Elizabeth Barrett was at last enjoying the stimulus of intellectual equality which had been missing from her secluded childhood and adolescence.

In 1837 her health broke down, her lungs were affected, and she was sent from London to the milder climate of Torquay. Her family took it in turns to stay with her there, and while her eldest brother Edward, nicknamed Bro, was prolonging his stay at Torquay at her entreaty, he went out sailing and was drowned. His sister's lasting grief altered and in some ways strengthened her character.

She came back to London in 1841, still very much of an invalid, and plunged into literary work—book reviews, articles, translations, contributions to symposia. This productive period culminated in the two-volume *Poems* of 1844, the most popular of all her works until *Aurora Leigh* with both the critics and the public. One poem in this collection, 'Lady Geraldine's Courtship', referred favourably to the work of Robert Browning, and he wrote to Elizabeth Barrett to thank her. So began, on 10 January 1845, a correspondence which led to their first meeting four months later. On the day after he had first seen Elizabeth Barrett, Browning sent her a declaration of love, which disturbed her so much that he had to disclaim it before she would consent to receive him again; and it was only gradually, with devoted patience, that he was able to convince her of the reality of his love, to make her avow hers, and to get her consent to an engagement. For a whole year they wrote to each other almost daily, sometimes twice a day, and he called on her every few days. More frequent visits would have aroused suspicion. Mr Barrett's immovable objection to the marriage of any of his children enforced secrecy on Browning and Elizabeth Barrett until they had left for Italy, a week after their marriage on 12 September 1846.

After some months in Pisa, the Brownings moved to Florence, which was to be their base for the rest of Mrs Browning's life; from 1848 they kept a permanent residence there, Casa Guidi, though they were often away from it for many months at a time, on visits to Rome, to Lucca, to Siena. In 1849 the poets' only child, a son christened Wiedeman, but afterwards nicknamed Pennini or Pen, was born. The Brownings visited London four times during the 1850s, and renewed their friendships in the literary world of London. They also spent two winters in Paris, where they got to know many French writers, and were witnesses of some of the most striking events in the rise to power of Napoleon III. Mrs Browning became increasingly absorbed in European politics, particularly the political development of Italy and France, and this preoccupation was reflected in the poetry which she wrote in the last ten years of her life. She also became deeply, almost obsessively, interested in spiritualism, though her credulity was tempered by occasional flashes of common sense.

In the 1840s and 1850s Elizabeth Barrett Browning's poetic reputation was at its height, and made her a serious candidate for the Poet Laureateship. The four books of poetry which she published between 1846 and 1861 were: the first collected edition of her poetry, published in 1850 and including, as well as the best of the 1838 and 1844 poems, some new lyrics and the celebrated 'Sonnets from the Portuguese', addressed to her husband; *Casa Guidi Windows*, a partly political poem about Italy, which appeared in 1851; *Aurora Leigh*, a modern epic or 'novel in verse', as she called it, which was published in 1857 and won immense acclaim; and *Poems before Congress*, 1860, again political in inspiration and deservedly less popular than any other work of her maturity. This was the last book which she published in her life-time. Her health, which had greatly improved with the happiness and the change of climate which her marriage and her move to Italy brought her, weakened again after she had reached the peak of her achievement in *Aurora Leigh*, and she died in Florence on 29 June 1861.

Her *Last Poems*, containing some of her most famous lyrics, were published posthumously in 1862. In the ensuing hundred years, many of her unpublished poems, especially her *juvenilia*, have appeared in small collections, and many volumes of her letters have been published in England and in America, where most of the surviving original letters are now. The most famous of these volumes of correspondence is her exchange of love letters with Robert Browning, a unique interplay of genius and passion. The best of the other collections of Elizabeth Barrett Browning's letters are those to R. H. Horne, Mary Russell Mitford, and Benjamin Robert Haydon, full of comment on contemporary literature, art and social problems; the letters to H. S. Boyd, chiefly concerned with Greek scholarship and metrical experiments; and the letters to her sister Henrietta and her brother George, which give a picture of her family and daily life. The best selection from her general correspondence is still Frederic Kenyon's two-volume one, published in 1898, though it necessarily omits a good deal of interesting biographical material which has appeared since then.

Even the baldest statement of the main events in Elizabeth Barrett Browning's life reveals an exceptional character and destiny. She was a fortunate woman. She had a happy childhood and, even after she grew up, a family life in which she never lacked affection, companionship and admiration for her talents, however much she was deprived of sympathetic understanding and of freedom. She experienced keen pleasure from the study of languages and literature, and had the leisure to indulge the taste fully. In middle life, when she seemed a confirmed invalid, she met and married a great poet who devotedly loved her. She had a charming and intelligent child; she lived in the most beautiful cities of Italy; she never experienced any real want of money; she had many devoted friends, who included most of the great writers of the day. She was convinced that she herself was born to be a poet, she was intensely happy writing poetry, and she had splendid success with her poems when they were published. She died without pain or lingering.

Her good fortune was due to the strength and integrity of her character as much as to her innate talents and her social and economic advantages. She had to overcome crippling ill-health, the loss of a dearly-loved brother, and the unforgiving tyranny and hardness of her father. To achieve this, and to make such a success of her personal and professional life, required a toughness of will, a generosity of heart, a healthiness of mind, which have not always been recognized in Elizabeth Barrett Browning, whose willpower and fierce mental energy have been somewhat obscured by her legend of invalidism and ringlets.

III

'A genuine poetess of no common order' said the *Examiner* of Elizabeth Barrett when reviewing *The Seraphim, and other Poems,* which was published in 1838 and widely praised. The title poem, a lyrical drama on the Crucifixion as seen through the eyes of two mourning archangels, is an ambitious unequal work full of imagination, of mystical visions of the red primaeval heats of creation still forever burning from the heavenly Throne and casting fiery shadows on the crystal sea; of the whole hierarchy of Heaven attendant on the hill of Golgotha:

> Beneath us sinks the pomp angelical,
> Cherub and seraph, powers and virtues, all,
> The roar of whose descent has died
> To a still sound, as thunder into rain.
> Immeasurable space spreads magnified
> With that thick life, along the plane
> The worlds slid out on.

The volume also contained several shorter poems such as 'A Deserted Garden', 'The Sleep', 'Cowper's Grave', which have always been popular with the anthologists. In this volume, too, appeared the first of the ballads which Elizabeth Barrett Browning's contemporaries loved best of all her works. Poems such as 'The Romaunt of Margret', 'Isobel's Child' and 'The Lay of the Brown Rosary' (which was published in 1844), in which the challenge between Love and Death is played out over and over again, with Death always triumphing, have a haunting Gothic strangeness and necromancy which is a persistent mood in nineteenth-century English poetry; from 'Christabel' and 'La Belle Dame Sans Merci' and 'The Lady of Shalott', it runs through Mrs Browning's ballads, and on from them to influence Rossetti's 'Sister Helen' and William Morris's 'The Blue Closet'.

Most of Elizabeth Barrett Browning's religious poetry also dates from the volume of 1838; not only 'The Seraphim', but such lyrics as 'The Soul's Travelling', 'The Virgin Mary to the Child Jesus' and 'Cowper's Grave', in which she meditated on mystical experiences and on the problem of reconciling belief in Divine Love with the suffering and the evils of the world, the problem which tormented so many of her contemporaries, above all Tennyson as he wrote *In Memoriam*. Most of these early religious poems of Mrs Browning's, though intense in feeling, are diffuse and undisciplined in expression, but in a few of the lyrics written at this time she achieved an economy of words which startles the reader by its fineness, as in 'My Doves', her poem about the imprisonment of city streets and the longing for escape. Most of the poem is musically sweet, rather than strong, as when she describes the cooing of the doves who share her imprisonment:

> Of living loves
> Theirs hath the calmest fashion,
> Their living voice the likest moves
> To lifeless intonation,
> The lovely monotone of springs,
> And winds, and such insensate things,

and then she surprises us with the unadorned fitness of her conclusion, in which, renouncing the hope of airy shores and silent dewy fields, she says:

> My spirit and my God shall be
> My seaward hill, my boundless sea.

This concentration is rare in her work; she achieved it in 'A Sabbath Morning at Sea', in 'A Seaside Walk', in snatches of 'The Poet's Vow' and 'Night and the Merry Men', but most completely in 'A Reed':

> I am no trumpet, but a reed,
> Go, tell the fishers, as they spread
> Their nets along the river's edge,

> I will not tear their nets at all,
> Nor pierce their hands, if they should fall;
> Then let them leave me in the sedge.

Elizabeth Barrett's next volume of poems, published in 1844, showed a development and hardening of her character and style. Illness, bereavement, approaching middle age, had made her less dreamy and more confident, even aggressive in her mannerisms. The 1844 volumes include her most advanced prosodic experiments, some of which seemed barbarous innovations to her contemporaries, but have many parallels in mid-twentieth-century poetry. Her political and social opinions were also growing more definite; two poems in the 1844 volumes, 'The Cry of the Children' and 'The Cry of the Human', were militant attacks on the employment of child labour in factories, and on the Protectionists who kept up the price of bread; the poems were widely commented on, and influenced public opinion in favour of reform. There is more intellect, and a more individual character, in the *1844 Poems* than in Elizabeth Barrett Browning's earlier works, and the volumes had a considerable success with the critics and the public; but in a good many of them there is a note of wildness and exaggeration which has caused subsequent literary historians to class Mrs Browning with the poets who were nicknamed the Spasmodic School, and were attacked for their over-strained hyperbole, subjectivism and lack of discipline. Two of the longer poems in Elizabeth Barrett's 1844 volumes— 'A Drama of Exile', a strange cloudy work on the expulsion of Adam and Eve from Paradise, and 'A Rhapsody of Life's Progress'—do almost justify her classification as a Spasmodic. But these same uneven volumes also contain some of her finest and most disciplined sonnets. Some, like 'Futurity' or the lapidary 'Grief', commemorate her brother's death and her struggle to accept her loss of him; some are analyses of the workings of poetic inspiration, like 'The Soul's Expression' and 'The Prisoner':

I count the dismal time by months and years,
Since last I felt the green sward under foot,
And the great breath of all things summer-mute
Met mine upon my lips. Now earth appears
As strange to me as dreams of distant spheres,
Or thoughts of Heaven we weep at. Nature's lute
Sounds on behind this door so closely shut,
A strange, wild music to the prisoner's ears,
Dilated by the distance, till the brain
Grows dim with fancies which it feels too fine,
While ever, with a visionary pain,
Past the precluded senses, sweep and shine
Streams, forests, glades,—and many a golden train
Of sunlit hills, transfigured to Divine.

One poem in the 1844 volumes, 'Catarina to Camoens', was a particular favourite with Robert Browning; he identified Elizabeth Barrett with the Portuguese girl Catarina, the beloved of the poet Camoens, and when his wife's sonnets to him were eventually published, the Brownings chose to call them 'Sonnets from the Portuguese', an ambiguous title which was a disguise from the world but full of secret meaning for the Brownings themselves. These sonnets were published in 1850, four years after the Brownings' marriage, in the first collected edition of Mrs Browning's works. The 'Sonnets from the Portuguese' are her best-known poems, but not her best. The dramatic story of her marriage has given the sonnets something of the fascination of a *roman à clef*, but considered simply as poetry they are unequal and sometimes embarrassing. Individual lines are strong and shapely:

Beholding, besides love, the end of love,
Hearing oblivion beyond memory,
As one who sits and gazes from above
Over the rivers to the bitter sea

or:

Yet love, mere love, is beautiful indeed,
And worthy of acceptation. Fire is bright

> Let temple burn, or flax. An equal light
> Leaps in the flame from cedar-plank or weed.

And there are some whole sonnets, notably xxii and xliii, which sustain an unforced strength of music. But it is impossible to say of the 'Sonnets from the Portuguese' as a whole, as one can say of the greatest sonnet sequences, that their beauty and interest is self-sufficing, independently of their personal reference. The abiding attraction of these sonnets is the psychological interest of tracing the evolution in love of a thirty-nine-year-old invalid, who at first cannot believe that a brilliant poet, six years younger than herself, can really love her and want to marry her; then, when she begins to believe it, is held back by conscientious scruples at burdening him with her melancholy and ill-health; then is brought to confess her own passion, and to see that he knows what he needs, and loves her for what she really is; then grows happy and luxuriates in the tokens and catchwords and secrets of acknowledged lovers; and at last looks forward to a life-time, an eternity, of enduring love.

Elizabeth Barrett Browning's marked individuality of style and personality makes all her poetry distinctive, but she was at various times much influenced by other poets. Pope was her model in her *juvenilia;* Campbell, Byron, Wordsworth, lent forms and themes to her early lyrics; and after her marriage to Browning, she acquired something of his powers of vivid ironic characterization and comment, an element in her poetry which had been latent since her earliest work but first came to the surface, under Browning's influence, in *Casa Guidi Windows*, published in 1851. This poem, written in a modified *terza rima*, is a reflection on recent political events in Florence and on the character and destiny of the Italians, about whom she is sympathetic but unsentimental:

> We chalked the walls with bloody caveats
> Against all tyrants. If we did not fight
> Exactly, we fired muskets up the air

To show that victory was ours of right.
We met, had free discussions everywhere
(Except perhaps i' the Chambers) day and night.
We proved the poor should be employed . . . that's fair,—
And yet the rich not worked for anywise,—
Pay certified, yet payers abrogated,—
Full work secured, yet liabilities
To over-work excluded.

Six years later, in 1857, she published her masterpiece, *Aurora Leigh*. This immense nine-book poem, longer than *Paradise Lost*, contains the finest passages that Elizabeth Barrett Browning ever wrote, but they are imbedded in an implausible story of a woman poet, a philanthropist who loves her, and a series of misunderstandings and catastrophes which keep them apart till the happy ending. The poem traces the parallel careers of Aurora Leigh, the successful but lonely and dissatisfied poet, convinced that man's salvation must come through the inspired individual, and her cousin Romney Leigh, the social reformer, who believes in progress organized for the people as a whole. He sets up a phalanstery on his ancestral estate, and decides to marry a poor seamstress as a precedent for a classless society. Romney's schemes fail—his bride is tricked away before the wedding, and entrapped into a brothel; the destitute people for whom he set up his phalanstery destroy it, and he loses his sight in the holocaust. When he and Aurora are finally reunited, they conclude that both were partly wrong; he had failed to recognize that to raise men's bodies you must first raise their souls; she had not seen that one must work with, as well as for, humanity.

Mrs Browning took various elements of the story of *Aurora Leigh* from Charlotte Brontë, George Sand and other novelists; but the best way to appreciate the poem is to disregard its story, and to read it—like Wordsworth's *Prelude*, which is perhaps its nearest affinity—not for the narrative, but for the reflections occasioned by the events in the narrative, for the glimpses of distant mountains, for the

moments of intense feeling. Elizabeth Barrett Browning
said that *Aurora Leigh* contained her highest convictions
on life and art, and in it she was above all concerned with the
poet's responsibilities, his call to be a witness to the values of
humanity. She was an early propagandist for *la littérature
engagée*, maintaining that the sole work of poets is

> to represent the age,
> Their age, not Charlemagne's,—this live throbbing age,
> That brawls, cheats, maddens, calculates, aspires,
> And spends more passion, more heroic heat,
> Betwixt the mirrors of its drawing-rooms,
> Than Roland with his knights at Roncesvalles.
> To flinch from modern varnish, coat or flounce,
> Cry out for togas and the picturesque
> Is fatal,—foolish too. King Arthur's self
> Was commonplace to Lady Guenevere;
> And Camelot to minstrels seemed as flat
> As Fleet Street to our poets.

Aurora Leigh is rich in unusual and glowing imagery,
mature and often witty in its comments on contemporary
society, compassionate over injustices and the sufferings of
the poor, and written in a vigorous and agile blank verse. It
had a great and immediate success, though some readers
were shocked by its frank sexual references, to prostitution
and even to rape. Mrs Browning was not a prude; she
thought that social evils were more likely to be abolished by
plain speaking about them than by pretending they did not
exist.

The last volume of poems which Mrs Browning published
in her lifetime, *Poems before Congress*, which appeared in
1860, was a disappointment. It was a small collection of
mainly political poems about France and Italy, too much
imbued with Mrs Browning's obsessive and often faulty
judgements on contemporary political events and person-
alities. A year after her death, a further small volume,
Last Poems, was published; it contained two lyrics, 'A

Musical Instrument' and 'The North and the South', which
have found their way into many anthologies, and one
remarkable poem, 'Bianca among the Nightingales', which
has a story and a refrain like some of the ballads of her youth,
but a passion and a sophistication which are quite new.

'*Last Poems* is the last title which anyone could desire to
read on a book which bears the name of Elizabeth Barrett
Browning', began the *Athenaeum* review of Mrs Browning's
posthumous volume, and it went on to call her 'the greatest
English poetess that has ever lived' and to say that she had
'the heart of a lion, the soul of a martyr, and the voice of a
battle-trumpet. Hers was a great genius, nurtured alike on
study of the ancients and instinct for the moderns.' Now, a
century later, no one would claim 'great genius' for Elizabeth
Barrett Browning, but there are qualities in her poetry
which still have power to move and interest us.

IV

Perhaps the best approach to the poetry of Elizabeth Barrett
Browning is to note first the thorough training and prepara-
tion she underwent in the techniques of her profession. It was
a profession to her; she worked full-time, all her adult life,
at the business of poetry, and she took seriously the skills
and the responsibilities of her trade. In writing of its responsibilities she sometimes lapsed into a shrill didacticism, but at
its best her vocation emerges as a genuine poetic impulse to
show life, and enable others to see it, as it really is, un-
obscured by prejudice, self-interest or self-deception.
Poets, she said, are 'the only truth-tellers still left to God',
and they must speak out against tyranny, against unjust
wars, against the exploitation of women and children,
against want and slavery, against complacency and ignorance.
They must make men think for themselves, must help them
to be honest about their emotions, must teach them to
outgrow narrow nationalism and sectarianism.

But if poets are to have the power to move men's minds in this way, they must learn the skills which give such power to poetry. She herself gave much time and study to the science of versification; she experimented in many different metres, and was a pioneer in the use of assonantal double rhymes. Her very thorough reading of English poetry, from the earliest to the latest, had convinced her that not enough use was made of the possibilities of rhyme. Double rhymes were almost confined to comic poetry; in any case, regular double rhymes were rare in English. Her innovation was to introduce such assonantal double rhymes as 'trident/ silent' and 'benches/influences', or still more extreme ones, matching neither in vowel nor consonant, such as 'angels/ candles' or 'burden/disregarding'. These are commonplaces in English poetry of the 1930s and 1940s, but in Mrs Browning's day, and for half a century afterwards, they were considered utterly lawless. Her metrical experiments were less extreme. She used a very wide variety of metres, from the most regular rhymed couplets and Petrarchan sonnets to the loosest accentual verse, approximating to sprung rhythm.

Her prosodic experiments were often more daring than successful, but they were the result of much exploration of Classical and Byzantine Greek literature and of early English poetry. She published a modernized version of a Chaucer poem, and translations of Aeschylus, Theocritus, Apuleius, Nonnus and Anacreon; she also wrote a critical study, illustrated by many translations, of Byzantine poetry from the fourth to the fourteenth century. Greek was the language she loved best, but she also knew Latin, French, Italian, and some German, Spanish and Hebrew, and was so widely read in the literature of these languages that she could trace an image from Lucretius through Saint Basil to Tasso, and draw a parallel between *The Choephoroe* and *Macbeth*, or between an ode of Anacreon and *Romeo and Juliet*. Some of the best known passages in her poetry are her roll-calls of other poets: in *An Essay on Mind*; in 'A Vision

of Poets', where she dashes off some notable sketches, such
as:

> Bold
> Electric Pindar, quick as fear,
> With race-dust on his cheeks, and clear
> Slant startled eyes that seem to hear
> The chariot rounding the last goal,
> To hurtle past it in his soul

and:

> Lucretius—nobler than his mood;
> Who dropped his plummet down the broad
> Deep universe, and said 'No God',
> Finding no bottom: he denied
> Divinely the divine;

and in *Aurora Leigh*, where she analyses the young poet's
reactions to his predecessors, how he loves and imitates them
and then finds his own inspiration, and how sometimes
there comes a poet like Keats, to whom none of the
generalizations about young poets apply; and then she wrote
the lines on Keats with which Edmund Blunden has chosen
to conclude his study of Keats in this series—

> the life of a long life
> Distilled to a mere drop, falling like a tear
> Upon the world's cold cheek to make it burn
> For ever.

Mrs Browning's knowledge of comparative literature
gave her an acute ear for style, and the boldness to refute, on
internal stylistic evidence and in an astonishing metaphor,
the theory of the multiple authorship of Homer. She pos-
sessed a handsome edition of Wolf's *Prolegomena ad
Homerum*, on thick white paper with wide margins, and she
wrote these memorably indignant lines about 'the kissing
Judas, Wolf':

> Who builds us such a royal book as this
> To honour a chief-poet, folio-built,

And writes above, 'The house of Nobody!',
Who floats in cream, as rich as any sucked
From Juno's breasts, the broad Homeric lines,
And, while with their spondaic prodigious mouths
They lap the lucent margins as babe-gods,
Proclaims them bastards. Wolf's an atheist;
And if the Iliad fell out, as he says,
By mere fortuitous concourse of old songs,
Conclude as much too for the universe.

The metaphor of the printed lines sucking the milk of the
white page-margins is a good example of another of
Elizabeth Barrett Browning's special poetic qualities—her
command of striking and original imagery. The richness of
her imagination is all the more surprising in view of how few
opportunities she had to observe either man or nature. She
spent the first twenty-five years of her life in the seclusion of
a remote countryside, and most of the next fourteen years
shut up in a London house, meeting very few strangers, and
ill in bed for whole years. But she made the fullest use of
what experience she had—of the conversation and letters of
her literary friends, of her long explorations and adventures
of the mind between the covers of books, even of her own
ill-health and its accompaniments. There is in her work a
whole image-cluster derived from her illness—from in-
somnia, from states of trance, from night silences and
transfigurations, from opium visions, from fainting, from
the vibrations of a galloping pulse. These made the landscape of her mind; they were to her what external nature
was to Wordsworth or Tennyson. She lived in the country
as a child, and she travelled widely after her marriage, but it
was mostly from one sofa to another. She led an indoor life,
and she writes like an indoor poet. Her descriptions of nature
often have the freshness of delighted surprise; trees and hills
and fresh air were to her not a necessity but a delicious
occasional stimulus, like going to the theatre. The spacious-
ness and dewy greenness of some of her landscape descriptions:

> The mythic oaks and elm-trees standing out
> Self-poised upon their prodigy of shade

remind one of the close dark room in which they were
written. What she actually saw from the window of her
room was the texture of the London skies—in winter
'wrapped like a mummy in a yellow mist', in summer 'a
thick mist lacquered over with light'; the sunsets which
'startle the slant roofs and chimney pots With splashes of
fierce colour' and the classic Dickensian spectacle, watching

> the great tawny weltering fog
> Involve the passive city, strangle it
> Alive, and draw it off into the void,
> Spires, bridges, streets, and squares, as if a sponge
> Had wiped out London,

surely a deliberate and ironic echo of Wordsworth's

> Ships, towers, domes, theatres and temples lie
> All bright and glittering in the smokeless air.

Mrs Browning's semantic studies often gave a special turn
to her imagery, an interlocking punning ambiguity, as in
her description of a man trying to rid himself of the ghost of
a dead love:

> He locks thee out at night into the cold
> Away from butting with thy horny eyes
> Against his crystal dreams,

where the adjective 'horny' is used in a double sense: the
eyes of the little ghost are horns to butt against a fragile
complacency, but also dim horn windows through which
an icy memory peers in. Mrs Browning concentrates and
interweaves her images so closely that they sometimes defy
analysis, and yet have a fierce impact:

> Ten nights and days we voyaged on the deep;
> Ten nights and days without the common face
> Of any day or night; the moon and sun

> Cut off from the green reconciling earth,
> To starve into a blind ferocity
> And glare unnatural; the very sky
> (Dropping its bell-net down upon the sea
> As if no human heart should 'scape alive)
> Bedraggled with the desolating salt.

This passage from *Aurora Leigh* describes how the orphan child, carried away from her home on a miserable voyage to a sad destination, sees all nature turned into the famished wild beasts of some cosmic circus, glaring through the net which has become man's prison, not his protection.

Another of Elizabeth Barrett Browning's special qualities, at once a virtue and a vice, is her great variety. She could plunge from heights of beauty to depths of bathos, sometimes within the same poem. But not all her good work is in one manner, and all her bad in another; even her best work is in several different manners. She could write with classic economy, as in her sonnet on hopeless grief:

> Most like a monumental statue set
> In everlasting watch and moveless woe,
> Till itself crumble to the dust beneath.
> Touch it: the marble eyelids are not wet;
> If it could weep, it could arise and go

or like her description of Michelangelo's statue of Lorenzo de' Medici:

> With everlasting shadow on his face,
> While the slow dawns and twilights disapprove
> The ashes of his long-established race,
> Which never more shall clog the feet of men.

Both these passages are inspired by sculpture, which was always one of Mrs Browning's most potent images; to her, as to Wordsworth, a statue was a 'marble index' of long voyages of the mind. But though she could write marmoreally, much of her most vivid poetry is more like a

modern sculptor's conglomeration of *objets trouvés*—
mechanisms and reptilian forms welded together in flowing
or glutinous structures; as in some passages from *Aurora
Leigh*:

> This social Sphinx
> Who sits between the sepulchre and the stews,
> Makes mock and mow against the crystal heavens,
> And bullies God

or:

> That June-day
> Too deeply sunk in craterous sunsets, now
> For you or me to dig it up alive,—
> To pluck it out all bleeding with spent flame
> At the roots, before those moralizing stars
> We have got instead

a passage which may recall ⌊to readers the poetry of
Christopher Fry, rather than of any nineteenth-century
writer.

Mrs Browning's learning and many interests, enriched by
the influence of her husband's still greater erudition, give her
poetry a very wide reference. Religion, philosophy,
politics, social reform, education, classical literature,
scientific discovery, all gave impulse to her poetic inspiration. Indignant at the chicanery of the Great Powers who
concluded the Peace of Villafranca, she dreams of

> the grand solution
> Of earth's municipal, insular schisms,
> Statesmen draping self-love's conclusion
> In cheap, vernacular patriotisms,
> Unable to give up Judaea for Jesus.

She draws a vivid image from the excavations at Pompei,
from Alexander's project to carve Mount Athos into a
colossal statue, from the holy ox of Memphis, from the
mixture of gall and potash on a painter's palette, from the
valves of a dissected hyacinth bulb. She reads Lyell's

Principles of Geology and Chambers's *Vestiges of the Natural History of Creation*, and is prompted to the reflection that

> Good love, howe'er ill-placed,
> Is better for a man's soul in the end,
> Than if he loved ill what deserves love well.
> A pagan, kissing for a step of Pan
> The wild-goat's hoof-print on the loamy down,
> Exceeds our modern thinker who turns back
> The strata . . . granite, limestone, coal and clay,
> Concluding coldly with 'Here's law! where's God?'

Often the imagery in her poetry can be traced back to references in her letters. These are now more read than her poetry, and would be more popular still if they were easily accessible in an up-to-date chronological arrangement. They are a barometer of the intelligent liberal public opinion of her times. Was it true that Newman had gone over to Rome? How long would it be before manhood suffrage was universal? Was Florence Nightingale really making the best use of her powers by being a hospital nurse? Could not prosperous Britain afford schools for all her children? In a letter of April 1846 she argues with Browning over the ethics of duelling. He has agreed with her in condemning capital punishment, and in opposing war, but yet he maintains that 'honourable men are bound to keep their honours clean at the expense of so much gunpowder and so much risk of life—*that* must be, ought to be—let judicial deaths and military glory be abolished never so!'. For her part, setting aside Christian principle, and on merely rational grounds, she 'cannot conceive of any *possible combination of circumstances* which could—I will not say *justify*, but even *excuse*, an honourable man's having recourse to the duellist's pistol, either on his own account or another's . . . His honour! Who believes in such an honour—liable to such amends, and capable of such recovery! *You* cannot, I think—in the secret of your mind. Or if *you can*—*you*, who are a teacher of the world—poor world—it is more desperately wrong than I thought'. When one finds Browning defending the principle of duelling as late as 1846, Pushkin's death in a duel only nine years earlier seems less strange.

Elizabeth Barrett Browning knew, in person or by correspondence, nearly all the eminent writers of her day, and read all the new books of any merit as they came out, and in her letters one can trace the rise and fall of reputations, the literary mysteries and controversies of the day. Could the author of *Adam Bede* really be a woman? How could anyone think Delavigne's poetry superior to Lamartine's, or Monckton Milnes's to Browning's? Could it possibly be true that *Jane Eyre* was by the governess of Thackeray's daughters? New names begin to rise in her literary firmament— Trollope's *Framley Parsonage* is 'really superb'; she is 'thunder-struck' by *Madame Bovary;* she had no idea that Thackeray had such intellectual force as *Vanity Fair* revealed; Matthew Arnold and Clough seem to her full of promise. In her letters one can also chart the rising temperature of her own fame; fan letters addressed to her simply as

Miss Elizabeth Barrett

Poetess

London

find their way to her in Wimpole Street; the terrible arbiters of the *Quarterly* and the *Examiner* begin to treat her with respect; her fellow poets write to congratulate her. But how was she to reply to a letter from Edgar Allan Poe hailing her as 'the noblest of her sex'? Perhaps she might say 'Sir, you are the most discerning of yours'.

This little joke, mocking herself as well as others, is typical of the personal style which makes Mrs Browning's letters, over and above the interest of many of their topics, so delightful. She had trained herself to write letters naturally, as though she were talking; they were indeed her only means of conversation for much of her life, when she was imprisoned by ill-health. And she had a rare ear and memory for the few face-to-face conversations which she did have, such as the misadventure of the Leeds poetess and the dropped H, which she recounted to Browning in a letter of May 1846.

A Miss Heaton had come to call, and had told Miss Barrett that 'the poetess proper of the city of Leeds was '*Mrs A*':

'Mrs A?' said I with an enquiring innocence.
'Oh' she went on, (divining sarcasm in every breath I drew) 'oh! I dare say, *you* wouldn't admit her to be a real poetess. But as she lives in Leeds, and writes verses, we call her our poetess! and then, really, Mrs A is a charming woman. She was a Miss Roberts—and her 'Spirit of the Woods', and of the 'Flowers' has been admired, I assure you'.
Well, in a moment I seemed to remember something,—because only a few months since, surely I had a letter from somebody who was once a spirit of the Woods or ghost of the Flowers. Still, I could not make out *Mrs A*!
'Certainly' I confessed modestly, 'I never did hear of a Mrs A.—and yet, and yet—' A most glorious confusion I was in, when suddenly my visitor thought of spelling the name 'H E-Y' said she. Now conceive that! The Mrs Iley who came by solution, had both written to me and sent me a book on the Lakes quite lately 'by the author of the Spirit of the Woods'. *There* was the explanation! And my Leeds visitor will go back and say that I denied all knowledge of the charming Mrs A. the Leeds poetess, and that it was with the greatest difficulty I could be brought to recognize her existence. Oh, the arrogance and ingratitude of me!'

This anecdote brings out the personality of Elizabeth Barrett—her ability to see herself as others saw her, her compassionate fear to wound competing with her irresistible sense of the absurd; a complex of qualities that made Henry James say 'there is scarce a scrap of a letter of Mrs Browning's in which a nameless intellectual, if it be not rather a moral, grace . . . does not make itself felt'. Elizabeth Barrett Browning's personality, as expressed in her writing, could be maudlin and over-excited; at other times she could be astringent and satirical; but she was not mean or sly. She had that magnanimity which, though it cannot be a substitute for talent, adds a grace to it. She was magnanimous in her freedom from all religious, national, class or sex prejudices, and magnanimous in her personal relationships. The greatest wrong she ever had to suffer was the selfish tyranny of her father, and here is what she said of it:

> After all, he is the victim. He isolates himself—and now and then he feels it . . . the cold dead silence all round, which is the effect of an incredible system. If he were not stronger than most men, he could not bear it as he does.

The complement to Elizabeth Barrett Browning's magnanimity, the final quality which distinguishes her poetry—and makes her resemble an Elizabethan poet such as Webster, or a modern one such as Dylan Thomas—is her outrageousness, the fearless unconcern with which she shouts and shocks and exaggerates. In real life she was a quiet-voiced gentle woman, a good listener rather than a good talker, but on paper she would say anything. Christian as she was, she would compare a waltz to the Mass, the unification of Italy to the Resurrection; no squeamishness prevented her from using scalps and tortures and rotting corpses as symbols; no prudery deterred her from talking of the smell of brothels. Like her prosodic experiments, these were deliberate attempts to create a new kind of poetic language, which would startle the reader into full participation. She often overdosed her poetry, and produced a lassitude rather than a stimulus in the reader. Her poems are not tasteful or aristocratic, and will never be appreciated by those who value restraint as a necessary element in good poetry. In thinking of her work, one is reminded of Roy Campbell's memorable lines:

> You praise the firm restraint with which they write—
> I'm with you there, of course;
> They use the snaffle and the curb all right,
> But where's the bloody horse?

Elizabeth Barrett Browning was not very handy with the snaffle or the curb, but the horse was there—a snorting and muscular charger, very liable to do a bolt.

V

In 1856 Ruskin said that Elizabeth Barrett Browning's poetry was 'unsurpassed by anything but Shakespeare'. In 1932 Virginia Woolf said that the only place in literature assigned to Mrs Browning was with Eliza Cook and Alexander Smith and other totally forgotten poets. Today, a century after Elizabeth Barrett Browning's death, her true worth as a poet is still unfixed between these extremes of critical inflation and deflation. Her poetry is very much out of favour with the academic critics and historians of literature. You will not find it among the set books in British university courses in English literature, nor in the latest anthologies. There is not a single poem of hers in John Hayward's *Penguin Book of English Verse* nor in W. H. Auden's *Poets of the English Language*, and a famous Professor is reported to have said that he could not find a poem of hers worth including in his anthology of English poetry. Not every public library in Britain has a copy of her works, and where copies do exist, they are not very often borrowed. No edition of the collected works is in print in Britain, though a new edition of 'Sonnets from the Portuguese' appeared in 1964. Elizabeth Barrett Browning's memory is kept alive at present more by the unending series of plays, films and musical comedies concerned with her private life than by readers of her poetry.

It is still too soon to say whether her fame as a poet will ever return. She may have to wait two hundred years, as Ford and Webster did till Charles Lamb brought them back to life. English literary taste moves in a circle, from extravagance to elegance and round again. It is possible that Elizabeth Barrett Browning's poetry will have a revival of favour at some future time when taste has followed its wonted cycle, and the terms 'gothic' and 'enthusiastic' have once again become terms of praise, not of abuse.

ELIZABETH BARRETT BROWNING
A Select Bibliography
(**Place** of publication London, unless stated otherwise)

Bibliography:

BIBLIOGRAPHY OF THE WRITINGS IN PROSE AND VERSE OF E. B. BROWNING, by T. J. Wise (1918)
—includes texts of some letters not published elsewhere, but lists as authentic Wise's forged 'Reading, 1847' edition of 'Sonnets [from the Portuguese]'

A BROWNING LIBRARY. A CATALOGUE OF PRINTED BOOKS, MANUSCRIPTS ETC. OF R. AND E. B. BROWNING, by T. J. Wise (1929)
—the catalogue of Wise's Browning collection, now in the British Museum.

BIBLIOGRAPHIES OF TWELVE VICTORIAN AUTHORS, by T. G. Ehrsam and R. H. Deily; New York (1936)
—Supplement by J. G. Fucilla in *Modern Philology*, XXXVII, 1939.

THE LIFE OF ELIZABETH BARRETT BROWNING, by G. B. Taplin (1957)
—contains a List of Principal Manuscripts Sources, and of Contributions to Annals, Almanacs, Periodicals and Series.

Collected Works:

POEMS. New edition. 2 vols (1850; 3 vols, 1856; 4 vols, 1864)
—the 1844 *Poems* with many additions, including for the first time 'Sonnets from the Portuguese'.

POEMS, with a prefatory note by R. Browning, 6 vols (1889)
—first published in 5 vols, 1866.

THE POEMS, with a memoir by Mrs D. Ogilvy (1893).

THE POETICAL WORKS, ed. F. G. Kenyon (1897).

THE POETICAL WORKS; Oxford (1904)
—first edition in the Oxford Standard Authors series.

COMPLETE POETICAL WORKS OF ELIZABETH BARRETT BROWNING, with introduction by L. Whiting. 2 vols; New York (1919).

POETICAL WORKS, WITH TWO PROSE ESSAYS (1920).

Selected Works:

A SELECTION FROM THE POETRY, with a prefatory note by R. Browning. First Series (1866). Second Series (1880).

POEMS, with an introduction by A. Meynell (1903).

SELECTED POEMS, edited with introduction and notes by E. Lee; Boston (1904).

POEMS (1912)
—in the World's Classics edition.

POEMS, selected with an introduction by S. J. Looker (1948).

Separate Works:

THE BATTLE OF MARATHON, A POEM. (1820).
—published anonymously.

AN ESSAY ON MIND, WITH OTHER POEMS (1826).
—published anonymously.

PROMETHEUS BOUND, TRANSLATED FROM THE GREEK OF AESCHYLUS, AND MISCELLANEOUS POEMS (1833)
—with an Introduction by A. Meynell, 1896

THE SERAPHIM, AND OTHER POEMS (1838).

THE POEMS OF GEOFFREY CHAUCER MODERNIZED (1841)
—Elizabeth Barrett contributed a version of 'Queen Annelida and False Arcite'.

POEMS. 2 vols (1844)
—by Elizabeth Barrett, Author of *The Seraphim* etc. This edition was used as the basis for subsequent editions of Elizabeth Barrett Browning's collected works produced in her lifetime and immediately after her death. The second edition, 1850, included much new material—a revised version of *Prometheus Bound*, the 'Sonnets from the Portuguese' (here published for the first time; the so-called 'Reading edition' of 1847 is a forgery), and 35 other sonnets and lyrics not previously published in book form. There was a third edition in 1853, a fourth (incorporating *Casa Guidi Windows*) in 1856 (in 3 vols), a fifth in 1862, a sixth (incorporating *Aurora Leigh*) in 1864, and a seventh, the final one, in 1866.

A NEW SPIRIT OF THE AGE, ed. R. H. Horne (1844)
—Elizabeth Barrett contributed a number of essays and parts of essays.

CASA GUIDI WINDOWS, A POEM (1851).

AURORA LEIGH (1857)
—with an Introduction by A. C. Swinburne, 1898.

POEMS BEFORE CONGRESS (1860)
—reprinted, New York, 1860, as *Napoleon III in Italy and Other Poems*.

LAST POEMS (1862).

THE GREEK CHRISTIAN POETS AND THE ENGLISH POETS (1863)
—articles reprinted from the *Athenaeum*, 1842; *The English Poets* being
a review of an anthology called *The Book of the Poets*.

PSYCHE APOCALYPTÉ, A LYRICAL DRAMA. Projected by E. B. Browning
and R. H. Horne (1876)
—an earlier draft of this was printed in *Hitherto Unpublished Poems*
(see below).

THE ENCHANTRESS, AND OTHER POEMS (1913).

EPISTLE TO A CANARY, ed. E. Gosse (1913).

LEILA, A TALE (1913).

NEW POEMS BY ROBERT BROWNING AND ELIZABETH BARRETT BROWNING,
ed. F. G. Kenyon (1914).

THE POET'S ENCHIRIDION, ed. H. B. Forman; Boston (1914).

HITHERTO UNPUBLISHED POEMS AND STORIES, WITH AN INEDITED AUTO-
BIOGRAPHY, ed. H. B. Forman. 2 vols; Boston (1914).

SONNETS FROM THE PORTUGUESE. Centennial Variorum Edition, edited
and with an introduction by F. Ratchford and notes by D. Fulton;
New York (1950)
—the 1856 text as finally revised by E. B. Browning, but with variant
readings from MS texts in the British Museum, Morgan Library and
Houghton Library.

Letters:

LETTERS ADDRESSED TO RICHARD HENGIST HORNE, ed. S. R. T. Mayer.
2 vols (1877).

KIND WORDS FROM A SICKROOM: [FOUR] LETTERS ADDRESSED TO ALLAN
PARK PATON; Greenock (privately printed, 1891).

LETTERS OF ELIZABETH BARRETT BROWNING, edited with biographical
additions by F. G. Kenyon. 2 vols (1897).

LETTERS OF ROBERT BROWNING AND ELIZABETH BARRETT, 1845-46.
2 vols (1899).

ELIZABETH BARRETT BROWNING IN HER LETTERS, by P. Lubbock (1906)
—a selection of the letters with critical commentary.

THE RELIGIOUS OPINIONS OF ELIZABETH BARRETT BROWNING: THREE
LETTERS ADDRESSED TO WILLIAM MERRY (1906)
—originally printed privately, 1896.

THE ART OF SCANSION: LETTER TO UVEDALE PRICE, with an introduction
by A. Meynell (1916).

LETTERS REPRINTED BY T. J. WISE (1916 and 1919).

LETTERS TO ROBERT BROWNING AND OTHER CORRESPONDENTS, ed. T. J.
Wise (privately printed, 1916).

ELIZABETH BARRETT BROWNING: LETTERS TO HER SISTER 1846-1859,
ed. L. Huxley (1929).

TWENTY-TWO UNPUBLISHED LETTERS OF ELIZABETH BARRETT BROWNING
AND ROBERT BROWNING, ADDRESSED TO HENRIETTA AND ARABELLA
MOULTON-BARRETT; New York (1935).

FROM ROBERT AND ELIZABETH BROWNING. A FURTHER SELECTION OF THE
BARRETT-BROWNING FAMILY CORRESPONDENCE, ed. W. R. Benet
(1936).

LETTERS TO BENJAMIN ROBERT HAYDON, ed. M. H. Shackford; New
York (1939).

TWENTY UNPUBLISHED LETTERS TO HUGH STUART BOYD, ed. B. Weaver
(1950).

ELIZABETH BARRETT TO MISS MITFORD: LETTERS TO MARY RUSSELL
MITFORD, edited and introduced by B. Miller (1954).

UNPUBLISHED LETTERS OF THOMAS DE QUINCEY AND ELIZABETH BARRETT
BROWNING, ed. S. Musgrove; Auckland (1954).

ELIZABETH BARRETT TO MR. BOYD: UNPUBLISHED LETTERS TO HUGH
STUART BOYD, edited and introduced by B. P. McCarthy (1955).

LETTERS OF THE BROWNINGS TO GEORGE BARRETT, ed. P. Landis and
R. E. Freeman; Urbana (1958).

BROWNING AND HIS AMERICAN FRIENDS: LETTERS BETWEEN THE
BROWNINGS, THE STORYS AND JAMES RUSSELL LOWELL, 1841-1890,
ed. G. R. Hudson (1965).

THE LOVE LETTERS OF ROBERT BROWNING AND ELIZABETH BARRETT, a
selection ed. with introduction by V. E. Stack (1969).

Some Biographical and Critical Studies:

A NEW SPIRIT OF THE AGE, by R. H. Horne (1844)
—contains a chapter on 'Miss E. B. Barrett and Mrs Norton'.

WORKS OF EDGAR ALLAN POE, ed. E. C. Stedman and G. E. Woodbury. Chicago (1895)
—Vol. VI contains an essay of 1845 on 'Miss Barrett's *A Drama of Exile, and other Poems*'.

NOTES SUR L'ANGLETERRE, by H. A. Taine; Paris (1872)
—includes a brief but important study of Mrs Browning's poetry.

TWO GREAT ENGLISHWOMEN: MRS BROWNING AND CHARLOTTE BRONTË, by P. Bayne (1881)
—critical study with a useful analysis of *The Seraphim* and 'A Drama of Exile'.

POÈTES MODERNES DE L'ANGLETERRE, by G. Sarrazin; Paris (1885)
—critical study.

ÉTUDES SUR MISTRESS ELIZABETH BROWNING, by C. des Guerrois; Paris (1885)
—analysis of Mrs Browning's aesthetic theory, and translations of some of the poems.

ELIZABETH BARRETT BROWNING, by J. H. Ingram (1888)
—the first biography, inaccurate as to some dates and facts, but sensible on poetry.

INTRODUCTION, by A. Meynell (1896)
—to edition of *Prometheus Bound and Other Poems*, E. B. Browning's first translation, originally published 1833.

INTRODUCTION to *Aurora Leigh*, by A. C. Swinburne (1898)

WILLIAM WETMORE STORY AND HIS FRIENDS, by H. James; Edinburgh (1903)
—includes some short but penetrating references to Mrs Browning.

THE BROWNINGS AND AMERICA, by E. P. Gould; Boston (1904)
—contains a survey of American reviews of E. B. Browning's poetry.

LA VIE ET L'OEUVRE D'E. B. BROWNING, by G. M. Merlette; Paris (1905)
—contains summaries and analyses of all principal poems, and a study of prosodic experiments.

THE BROWNINGS, THEIR LIFE AND ART, by L. Whiting (1911)
—the first authoritative biography; many of the facts were obtained from the Brownings' son.

ENGLISH SONGS OF ITALIAN FREEDOM (1911) and ENGLISHMEN AND
ITALIANS: SOME ASPECTS OF THEIR RELATIONS PAST AND PRESENT (1919)
by G. M. Trevelyan
—assesses E. B. Browning's influence on political opinion.

FEMME ET POÈTE: ELISABETH BROWNING, by R. B. Nicati; Paris (1912)
—critical study, includes analysis of E. B. Browning's religion.

ELISABETTA BARRETT BROWNING, by B. Viterbi; Bergamo (1913)
—biography.

THE BROWNINGS, by O. Burdett (1928)
—critical study.

ELIZABETH BARRETT BROWNING, by L. S. Boas (1930)
—biography.

THE COMMON READER, Second Series, by V. Woolf (1932)
—the most important critical study by a 20th-century creative writer.

FLUSH, by V. Woolf (1933)
—ostensibly a biography of E. B. Browning's dog, but contains
biographical material on her.

AN ENQUIRY INTO THE NATURE OF CERTAIN NINETEENTH CENTURY
PAMPHLETS, by J. Carter and G. Pollard (1934)
—exposes the 1847 edition of the Sonnets from the Portuguese as a
forgery.

ELIZABETH BARRETT BROWNING: R. H. HORNE: TWO STUDIES, by M. H.
Shackford; Wellesley, Mass. (1935)
—critical study.

THE FAMILY OF THE BARRETT, by J. Marks; New York (1938)
—history of the Barrett family in Jamaica. Section on E. B. Browning's
opium addiction.

THE IMMORTAL LOVERS, by F. Winwar (1950)
—biography.

ELIZABETH BARRETT BROWNING, by D. Hewlett (1953)
—biography and critical study.

ROBERT ET ELIZABETH BROWNING, by A. Maurois; Paris (1955)
—the best representative of the disillusioned view of the Brownings'
story.

THE GOLDEN RING: THE ANGLO-FLORENTINES, by G. A. Treves (1956)
—section on the Brownings' lives and friends in Florence.

THE LIFE OF ELIZABETH BARRETT BROWNING, by G. B. Taplin (1957)
—biography, incorporating much new material; valuable bibliography.

AURORA LEIGH, the Fawcett Lecture, by J. M. S. Tompkins (1961)
—analyses E. B. Browning's ideas on women as writers.

MRS BROWNING: A POET'S WORK AND ITS SETTING, by A. Hayter (1963)
—critical study.

A SULTRY MONTH: SCENES OF LONDON LITERARY LIFE IN 1846, by
A. Hayter (1964).

OPIUM AND THE ROMANTIC IMAGINATION, by A. Hayter (1968)
—contains a chapter about Mrs Browning as an opium taker.

Note: Important material on E. B. Browning is contained in Robert
Browning's letters and in biographies of him:

RECORDS OF TENNYSON, RUSKIN AND THE BROWNINGS, by Lady Ritchie
[Anne Isabella Thackeray] (1892).

ROBERT BROWNING, by G. K. Chesterton (1903).

LIFE AND LETTERS OF ROBERT BROWNING, by Mrs S. Orr (1908).

LIFE OF ROBERT BROWNING, by W. H. Griffin and H. C. Minchin (1910).

LETTERS OF ROBERT BROWNING, ed. T. L. Hood (1933).

ROBERT BROWNING AND JULIA WEDGWOOD. A BROKEN FRIENDSHIP AS
REVEALED IN THEIR LETTERS, ed. R. Curle (1937).

NEW LETTERS OF ROBERT BROWNING, ed. W. C. de Vane and K. L.
Knickerbocker (1951).

DEAREST ISA. ROBERT BROWNING'S LETTERS TO ISABELLA BLAGDEN, ed.
E. C. McAleer; Austin, Texas. (1951).

ROBERT BROWNING, A PORTRAIT, by B. Miller (1953).

AMPHIBIAN: A RECONSIDERATION OF BROWNING, by H. C. Duffin (1956).

ROBERT BROWNING AND HIS WORLD; THE PRIVATE FACE, by M. Ward
(1968).